FAITH HILL

by
Jill C. Wheeler

Visit us at
www.abdopub.com

Published by ABDO & Daughters, an imprint of ABDO Publishing Company, 4940 Viking Drive, Edina, MN 55435.

Printed in the United States.

Graphic Design: John Hamilton
Cover Design: Mighty Media
Cover photo: Corbis
Interior photos:
AP/Wide World, p. 5, 7, 9, 27, 31, 32, 37, 38, 41, 43, 45, 46, 49, 51, 52, 54, 57, 59, 60
Corbis, p. 1, 10, 12, 14, 17, 19, 20, 23, 24, 28, 35, 62

Library of Congress Cataloging-in-Publication Data

Wheeler, Jill C., 1964-
Faith Hill / Jill C. Wheeler.
p. cm. — (Star tracks)
Includes index.
Summary: Profiles the music star who was the first female country singer ever to achieve double platinum status on both her debut and follow-up albums.
ISBN 1-57765-771-3
1. Hill, Faith, 1967—Juvenile literature. 2. Country musicians—United States—Biography—Juvenile literature. [1. Hill, Faith, 1967- 2. Singers. 3. Country music 4. Women—biography.] I. Title. II. Series

ML3930.H53 W54 2002
782.421642'092—dc21
[B]

2001045991

CONTENTS

DREAMS DO COME TRUE

WHEN PEOPLE THINK OF THE GRAND OLE Opry near Nashville, Tennessee, they think of country music. Since 1925, the Opry has hosted a weekly radio broadcast featuring the best music from new and established country artists. In fact, some people credit the Opry with popularizing country music across the nation.

Everybody who's anybody in country music has at sometime sung on stage at the Grand Ole Opry. Likewise, anybody who wants to become somebody in country music dreams of doing the same. Faith Hill is no exception. Since she was a child, she had dreamed of the time when she, too, would sing at the Opry.

That dream came true on March 2, 1993. The tall, beautiful 25-year-old singer walked on stage and sang two songs. That's about all she remembers. "I was just numb," she said later. "I was out there for two songs, walked off the stage, and I swear I can't tell you anything about it."

Hill had just signed a recording contract and had not yet released her first album. She was new to the glamour and lights of professional singing. Yet it wouldn't be long before she would be performing and touring like a seasoned pro.

Since then, Hill has taken the country music industry by storm. Within six years she has sold more than 11 million albums. She's received virtually more honors and awards than anyone can count. The rapid rise of her career has shattered old records and set new ones. In fact, she became the first female country singer ever to achieve double-platinum status on both her debut and follow-up albums.

Behind the success is a hard-working artist with a soft heart. Hill is a perfectionist, demanding the most out of herself both on stage and in the studio. She's also willing to give of herself, and her talents, to make the world a better place. Most recently, Hill has become one of the hardest-working mothers in country music.

Behind Faith Hill's success is a hard-working artist with a soft heart.

Hill performs because she loves to. Her fans love her because she never forgets who she's performing for. "There's got to be something for the fans to connect to in order for them to go out and spend their hard-earned money on a Faith Hill recording," she said. "I'm constantly thinking about them. I hope they realize that and like the direction that I'm going."

Faith Hill sings the national anthem before the start of Super Bowl XXXIV in Atlanta, Georgia, on January 30, 2000.

THE STAR FROM STAR

FAITH HILL WAS BORN ON SEPTEMBER 21, 1967, in Jackson, Mississippi. Faith's biological mother was an unmarried teenager who gave her up for adoption. Pat and Edna Perry from nearby Star, Mississippi, were delighted to adopt the baby. They named her Audrey Faith Perry.

Faith joined the Perry's two sons: Wesley, eight, and Steve, five. It was tough for her father, who worked in a manufacturing plant, and her mother, a bank employee, to feed another mouth. However, they agreed that having baby Faith in the family was worth the extra work. "My mother wanted a girl, my dad didn't," Faith recalled. "She finally talked him into adopting me. Once I was theirs, my dad was putty in my hands."

Faith Hill accepts her award for favorite female musical performer at the 27th Annual People's Choice Awards, January 7, 2001.

The Perrys provided Faith with a solid, loving family. She always knew she was adopted, and she always felt fortunate to have been brought into the family. "They were strong, the hardest-working people I've ever known," Faith said of her parents. "Mom financially stretched a dollar into 10. My parents' combined salary when I left home at 18 was probably $25,000, raising three kids and paying bills. That's impressive."

Faith's father had been one of 13 children growing up in a poor family. He quit school in the fourth grade so he could help earn money for his family. As a result, he never learned to read beyond the fourth-grade level. Despite that handicap, he successfully raised a family and worked stable jobs all his life. Faith remembers that he was always there for her, no matter what.

The Perrys raised their children with small-town values and solid Christian faith in God. They encouraged their children to try new things and supported them whether or not their efforts worked out. "My mom has always, always taught me to keep my feet on the ground in whatever I did," Faith said. "The things when I was in school, things that I won, talent shows or whatever, to her it was most important that I kept my head screwed on straight."

Faith always tried to keep up with her older brothers. In doing so, she often ended up dirty, scraped, and bruised. Once she perched on the handlebars of her brother's bicycle while he was riding it. Her foot accidentally got caught in the spokes, sending her flying. She wound up in the emergency room, but recovered quickly.

With a loving family behind her, Faith grew up self-confident and strong. She grew to be five feet, nine inches tall. Like many young women, she had occasional worries about her appearance. She was tall and lanky and had braces for awhile. She even admits that when she was younger, she wanted to be just five feet, five inches tall.

But Faith didn't let those worries hold her back. She became a cheerleader as well as a basketball star. Her classmates elected her president of her junior class at McLaurin Attendance Center. As one of her friends recalled, "Faith never did anything halfway. In cheerleading she didn't just chant, she screamed." Faith agreed. "I was very independent, and when I had my mind set on doing anything, I thought I was going to do it."

Also like many young people, Faith had a rebellious side. There wasn't much to do in the small town of Star. Faith recalls that it was a very simple town. "A couple of churches, a gas station, and a school. That's it," she said. She and her friends found their own unique ways to rebel, like spreading toilet paper around neighbors' yards and speeding through railroad crossings in her car. "I was fearless," she said. "I enjoyed doing crazy, daredevil things… . I wasn't a hoodlum or anything, but I liked to get in trouble a little bit, to see how far I could go." She feels her parents did a good job of allowing her to explore, but not go too wild.

"I liked to get in trouble a little bit, to see how far I could go."

FLEDGLING SONGBIRD

FAITH BEGAN TO SING ALMOST AS SOON as she began to talk. She sang in public for the first time when she was about three years old. "My mother said that I held the hymnal upside-down and sang as loud as I could, pretending I could read the words off the book," Faith said. She joined the youth choir while still in grade school, and was allowed to sing in the adult choir at age 16.

Church music was the first music Faith ever heard, and she loved it. Her favorite memories are of when the youth choir traveled during the summer. She claims those trips were when she cut her "musical teeth." She eventually came to know and enjoy the gospel music of African Americans. "People were on their feet the entire time in those churches," she said. She knew from childhood that someday she wanted to be an entertainer.

Faith often sang at family gatherings, and around age 10, she sang at the local 4-H club mother-daughter luncheon. She always loved singing, but sometimes she was shy about singing around other people. It was then that her mother would bribe her with quarters. Then she'd sing songs like Tanya Tucker's 1972 hit "Delta Dawn," or church songs like "Jesus Loves Me."

At age 13, Faith began teaching herself how to play the guitar. Around age 17, she joined a band and began performing at local fairs, rodeos, and private parties. They played traditional country music, as well as gospel.

One of the strangest places Faith ever performed was at a "tobacco spit" in Raleigh, Mississippi. At the event, people stood on one end of a stage that had spittoons at either end. The people chewed tobacco, and then had to spit the tobacco juice across the stage and into one of the spittoons. "It was really, really gross," Faith said. "They cleaned the stage off with towels, and then I went on. I remember standing up there going, 'Oh, God, what is this?' But I was still grateful to be there. It was another opportunity to perform."

While Faith's first musical exposure was to gospel, rhythm and blues (R&B) soon followed. Aretha Franklin and Elvis Presley were two of her favorites. The first music album she ever owned was Elvis's *A Legendary Performer Volume Two*. In 1975, she got to see him in concert.

Faith's true love, however, was country music. As a youngster she enjoyed George Jones, Tammy Wynette, and Patsy Cline. Later, she became a huge fan of Reba McEntire. "I remember coming home after school and playing her records in my room over and over until it was time for supper," Faith said of McEntire. She also admitted to having a crush on George Strait.

After graduating from high school in 1985, Faith enrolled at Hinds Community College in Raymond, Mississippi. Yet her mind was never completely on her studies. She finally had to admit to her family that she wanted to be a country music singer, not an employee at a nine-to-five job. With her parents' support, she quit school and moved to the heart of the country music world—Nashville, Tennessee.

NASHVILLE

FOR THE NEXT FEW YEARS, FAITH WORKED a series of odd jobs in Nashville. Her first job there was selling T-shirts at the Country Music Fan Fair. Fan Fair is an annual event that gives country music fans an opportunity to hear and even meet their favorite country music artists. Another of her jobs was working for the fan club of her idol, Reba McEntire. McEntire recalls working with the young woman. "Faith was a bright, spunky, feisty girl," she said. "Real sweet and open, but a little mischievous. She reminded me a lot of myself."

Faith later got a job working as a receptionist for music publisher Gary Morris Music. Ironically, Faith only got the job because she pretended she didn't want to become a singer. And while she didn't enjoy being a receptionist, she did learn about the music business from the inside. "I got to see sides of the business that I never even thought existed," she said.

Working in Nashville, Faith began to meet people in the music industry. One of them was music publishing executive and aspiring songwriter Daniel Hill. He and Faith began dating in the spring of 1987. They were married on July 23, 1988.

Meanwhile, Faith kept her sights focused on a career in music. She finally got a break around 1990, when a songwriter heard her singing when she thought no one was listening. The songwriter, David Chase, encouraged Faith to record a demo of a song. She did, and Chase eventually played the song for Gary Morris himself. Morris told Faith to get away from the receptionist desk and get singing.

Faith took Morris's advice. She soon found herself a gig singing back-up with Gary Burr. The two ended up singing regularly at Nashville's Bluebird Café. It was there that Faith's voice came to the attention of Martha Sharp. Sharp was a talent scout for Warner Bros. A&R. She had been the first person to spot Randy Travis. Now, she added Faith Hill to her list of finds. Faith soon signed a record contract with Warner Bros. Records.

SEARCHING FOR A PAST

ABOUT THE TIME SHE SIGNED HER FIRST contract, Hill decided to try to find her birth parents. She had always been happy in the Perry family. Yet she remained curious about her biological parents.

"I was so ambitious as a child," she said. "I was a dreamer, the kind of dreams that made me know things were going to happen for me. So I always wondered where that quality came from. And there are all those other questions: Who do I look like? Do I have a brother? Do I have a sister? So I went on a search, but I didn't begin it without the support of my family."

Hill's search took three years. Finally, in 1993, she located her biological mother, who turned out to be a painter—and tall, just like Hill.

"The first time I met my biological mother, I just stared at her," she said. "I'd never seen anybody who looked anything like me."

While Hill considers the Perrys her real family, she still sees her biological mother from time to time, as well as her biological brother. Sadly, she learned her biological father had died several years before her search began.

"I was a dreamer, the kind of dreams that made me know things were going to happen for me."

WRITING A FUTURE

MEETING HER BIRTH MOTHER WAS A VERY emotional event for Hill. Some people say it contributed to the problems she was having in her marriage with Daniel Hill. "I was young," she said of her first marriage. "I just jumped in the fire way too soon." The two divorced in 1994. The intense emotions she was feeling appear in songs she was working on for her first album, *Take Me As I Am*.

Warner Bros. Records released the album in the fall of 1993. In January 1994, the debut single "Wild One" shot to the top of the *Billboard* magazine country singles charts. It stayed there for four weeks. The song made Hill the first female country artist in 30 years whose debut single held a spot at the top for such a long time. The second single from the album, "Piece of My Heart," also reached the number one spot. Eventually *Take Me As I Am* went double-platinum, selling two million copies.

Faith Hill at a 1995 performance in Nashville, Tennessee.

A platinum album is rare for a brand-new artist. Not surprisingly, the music industry took note of Hill's accomplishment. In 1993, officials of the Academy of Country Music named her their top new female vocalist, and she earned honors from *Billboard* magazine as new country artist of the year.

Soon afterward, Hill went on a challenging 150-date tour. It was a dream come true. Hill found herself touring with the same country superstars she'd listened to as a teen, like Reba McEntire and her old crush George Strait. The downside of appearing with such names was that she was often the opening act. Many concert-goers are impatient with opening acts. They are only there to see the main star. When Hill opened for Strait, there were nights that she nearly left the stage in tears because the audience wouldn't respond to her.

Toward the end of her touring, Hill realized she had a problem. Doctors discovered she had an enlarged blood vessel in her throat. Hill had to admit she had been singing too much, giving too many interviews, and performing in smoky clubs. A singer's voice needs to be cared for like any important tool. But Hill had never received formal vocal training to help her voice stand up to the demands of a concert tour. She underwent surgery, and then was not allowed to speak for two weeks. She took another three months off to recover.

While working on *Take Me As I Am*, Hill had become friends with music producer Scott Hendricks. Their relationship deepened as time went by. Finally, on Valentine's Day 1995, he asked her to marry him. Hill had just had her surgery and couldn't talk. Instead, she nodded "Yes."

A singer's voice needs to be cared for like any important tool.

WHAT REALLY MATTERS

AS SOON AS HILL'S THROAT HEALED, SHE and Hendricks were back in the recording studio. Hill felt a lot of pressure. After the success of her debut album, she couldn't afford to let her fans down with a poor follow-up. She was also worried about her voice. Would she be able to do it?

Fortunately for her fans, Hill's voice was better than ever. Her second album, *It Matters To Me,* came out in 1995 and went on to become triple-platinum. The title track also climbed to number one on the country charts. And she went back on tour, this time opening for her friend Alan Jackson.

In March 1996, with Jackson's tour behind her, Hill took on a new touring gig with country star Tim McGraw. The Spontaneous Combustion tour would become the stuff of legends. More than a million fans in nearly every state would see it, making it one of the highest-grossing tours of the year.

Faith Hill and Tim McGraw arrive at the 35th Annual Academy of Country Music Awards *in Universal City, California, May 3, 2000.*

Faith Hill and husband Tim McGraw at the Country Music Association Awards *in Nashville, Tennessee, September 22, 1999.*

Country songs are often about romance. Frequently, they're done as duets with a man and a woman. During the Spontaneous Combustion tour, the show's producers paired Hill with McGraw for a duet. The two had met briefly several years before, but they didn't know each other well. As the tour wore on, that changed. Audiences were the first to see that the tour's real spontaneous combustion was between Hill and McGraw.

"It was just one of those things that was going to happen," Hill said of her falling in love with McGraw on the tour. "It was destiny. I know that sounds trite, but it was really true." Hill broke off her engagement with Scott Hendricks and on October 6, 1996, she married McGraw in the Louisiana town he had lived in as a young child. Hill regretted having to break an engagement. "But I wasn't about to let Tim slip through my hands," she said.

A QUEST FOR LITERACY

DURING THE SPONTANEOUS COMBUSTION tour, Hill started a new personal mission. She had never forgotten how difficult it had been for her father to get through life unable to read well. She wanted to help prevent other people from having that same disadvantage. Hill worked with Time Warner and her record label, Warner Bros. Records, to found the Faith Hill Family Literacy Project. The project educates people about illiteracy and encourages them to support literacy projects in their communities. Hill has said that her dream is "that someday every American will be able to read."

When Hill undertook her first solo tour in 1999, she took her quest for literacy on the road with her. She asked her fans to bring new or used books to her concerts for donation to hospitals, day care centers, schools, and libraries.

Hill received help from America's Promise, a service group led by U.S. General Colin Powell. With that group's help, Hill collected and distributed more than 25,000 books over the course of her tour.

In the fall of 1996, Hill also worked on two children's album projects. They were called *Country Disney: The Best of Country Sings the Best of Disney,* and *For Our Children, Too*. Part of the proceeds from *For Our Children, Too* went to the Pediatric AIDS Foundation. August 1996 saw another special honor for Hill. She was invited to sing at the closing ceremonies of the Summer Olympic Games in Atlanta, Georgia. That December, Faith gave a nationally televised performance at the annual "Christmas in Washington" celebration.

Around this time, Hill and McGraw also recorded the song "It's Your Love" for his new album. The single spent six weeks at the top spot on the country charts. And the couple had been working on another special joint project. Gracie Katherine was born in May 1997.

Faith Hill and husband Tim McGraw perform together at the International Country Music Fan Fair *festival in Nashville, Tennessee, June 17, 1997.*

FROM COUNTRY TO POP STAR

HILL DECIDED TO TAKE SOME TIME AWAY from the studio and stage after Gracie's birth. "My career had been really busy," she said. "There were so many things going on that I just wasn't feeling... creative anymore... . I needed to live a little bit, get off the road." To stretch her horizons, that fall she made appearances on episodes of TV shows *Touched By An Angel* and *Promised Land*.

After a short leave, Hill returned to the recording studio to finish her third album—her first in three years. She was nervous about returning to the studio after so much time. Hill need not have worried. Something about taking time off and having a child had made her voice even stronger than before.

MOTOR
HARLEY-DAVIDSON
CYCLES

Faith Hill holds her daughter Gracie as she performs July 22, 1998, at the Adams County FairFest '98 *in Hastings, Nebraska. Hill performed to a sold out audience despite being almost nine months pregnant.*

The album was called *Faith* and it hit the stores in April 1998. Hill said the title of the album referred more to her growth as an artist than to her name. She'd always had to have faith that things would work out. And they did. Not only was her third album a success, but Hill also gave birth to her second daughter, Maggie Elizabeth, in August of 1998.

Faith's first single, "This Kiss," quickly climbed the *Billboard* magazine charts—both the country singles chart and the Hot 100 pop charts. "This Kiss" spent three weeks at the top of the country chart and peaked at number seven on the pop chart. *Faith* was the first crossover success for Hill and it went multiplatinum. Songs from the album appear on the soundtracks for the movies *The Prince of Egypt*, *Message in a Bottle*, and *Pearl Harbor*.

Hill followed *Faith* with *Breathe* in November 1999. It too sold more than three million copies. The title track hit number one on *Billboard* magazine's country singles and adult contemporary charts. The song and album also netted Hill Grammy Awards for best female country vocal performance and best country album.

Some music critics thought *Breathe* was more of a pop album than a country album. Hill said she hadn't planned on it being either way. She said the album was just a matter of her being who she was. "I can only do what's real to me," Hill said. "I couldn't go out and make a pop record if I tried. And I couldn't go out and make a traditional country record, either, because I'm inspired by too many things—deep gospel, R&B, soul."

While *Breathe* did upset some traditional country fans, it also made Hill's star rise among pop audiences. Plus, she felt the album reflected a lot of herself. "The music that I make has to be right for me at the right time," she said. "It has to have meaning." The title track definitely reflects the intensity of Hill's career. In addition, the album features the passionate duet with husband Tim McGraw that captured Hill's third Grammy Award.

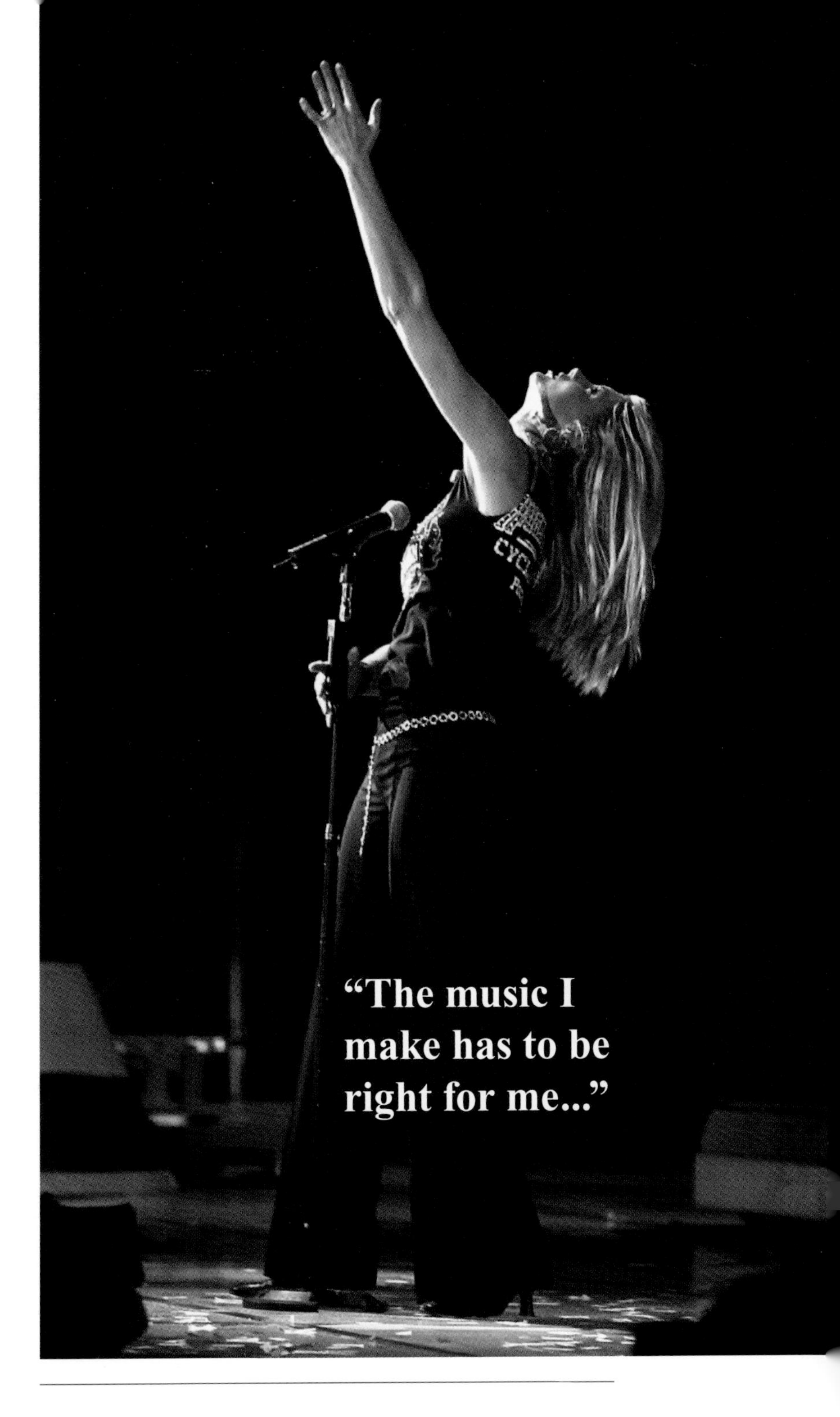
"The music I make has to be right for me..."

ON THE ROAD

BEING A WIFE AND MOTHER HAS MADE Hill's career both more challenging and more rewarding. She insists on taking her daughters with her when she tours, despite the inconveniences. They travel in a specially designed bus packed with all the things that accompany life with children. "We have multiples of everything," Hill said. "The same car seats, blankets, the same toys, so they don't miss out on their favorite things at home altogether."

Hill has her husband and a nanny to help her with the children. However, she takes pride in taking on as much of the parenting responsibility as she can. One of her back-up singers says she's seen Hill change a diaper three minutes before she walked on stage.

Faith Hill gets close to her fans during the 1995 International Country Music Fan Fair *in Nashville, Tennessee.*

Faith Hill holds her award for best country album at the 28th Annual American Music Awards, *January 8, 2001.*

Hill and McGraw have also made special arrangements to keep their relationship strong. When they married, they agreed never to be separated for more than three days. Sometimes that means long plane rides for just a few hours together in between shows. Both say it's worth it.

Other times, the family ties mean lost opportunities. "I had a chance to tour Europe, where 'This Kiss' was huge," Hill said. "But it would've meant being away from my daughters for three weeks, and I didn't want to do that. Actually, it wasn't a hard decision. I think it was a lot more difficult for my record company than it was for me."

"I've always wanted a family as much as I've wanted my career," Hill said. "I won't lie: it is a lot of work, and I'm tired… but we learned how to pack and get around and do what we have to do. It's amazing what you can wake up every morning and accomplish as long as you're happy."

The situation was ideal, however, in 2000. The Hill-McGraw powerhouse hit the road for the Soul 2 Soul Tour 2000. The sold-out show was one of the top country tours of the year. It also gave the family a chance to be together all the time. Both Hill and McGraw can't say enough how important their family is to their musical success.

"Becoming a wife and a parent really changes everything," Hill said. "Being a mother has inspired me in every part of my life including my music." She adds that marrying McGraw was the best thing she ever did. "Tim has given me confidence and strength and my foundation," she said. "He makes me feel like I can conquer the world."

Faith Hill and Tim McGraw perform together at the 35th Annual Academy of Country Music Awards, *May 3, 2000.*

BRANCHING OUT

IF HILL HASN'T YET CONQUERED THE world, she's on her way. In addition to her music, she's become a popular spokesperson. She's signed contracts with Pepsi and Alltel (a telecommunications firm). In 1999, she signed a contract with Cover Girl Cosmetics to be a new model in their advertising campaign. Few people were surprised. Hill had already been singled out by *People* magazine as one of their 50 Most Beautiful People. However, the Cover Girl model admits makeup isn't her favorite thing. "I don't like to wear makeup unless I absolutely have to," she said.

Hill continues to pile up awards from the Country Music Association and the Academy of Country Music, as well as some pop honors. In April 1999, she appeared on the popular *VH1 Divas Live* series. In 2000, she sang the national anthem for Super Bowl XXXIV, and appeared at the Academy Awards.

Faith Hill accepts her Female Artist of the Year award at the TNN & CMT Country Weekly Music Awards *show in Nashville, Tennessee, June 13, 2001.*

In December 2001, Hill was a part of the *America: A Tribute to Heroes* telethon, which raised $150 million for people involved in the September 11 terrorist attacks.

When not on the road, she, McGraw, and the girls have a six-bedroom colonial-style house outside Nashville to call home. And, their home has a new resident. Audrey Caroline was born on December 6, 2001.

For the future, Hill says she hopes to reduce her touring. She also hopes to combine her music with a more "normal" existence. When asked what she'd like to be doing in 10 years, she lists the kind of balance people have come to expect from Faith Hill. "I'd like to have recorded a Christmas album and several more albums, period. I'd like to do a movie if the right thing came along… And I'd like to watch my children grow and, you know, grow a garden."

In the present, however, Hill remains happy, upbeat, and slightly awed by how her life has turned out. "It feels incredible," she said. "A lot of the places of my dreams are even better than what I imagined."

Tim McGraw gives Faith Hill a hug and kiss prior to the start of rehearsal of his number one single "Please Remember Me" during the 34th Academy of Country Music Awards *show rehearsal, May 3, 1999.*

Faith Hill and Tim McGraw show off their awards at the 43rd Annual Grammy Awards, *February 21, 2001.*

GLOSSARY

debut: a first appearance.

literacy: being able to read and write.

platinum: an album that sells more than one million copies. A double-platinum album has sold more than two million, and so on.

single: one song from an album, sold by itself.

spittoon: a container to hold spit.

WEB SITES

Would you like to learn more about Faith Hill? Please visit **www.abdopub.com** to find up-to-date Web site links about Faith Hill and her music career. These links are routinely monitored and updated to provide the most current information available.

INDEX